THE GALAXY GUIDES

WHY IS THE MOON NOT A PLANET?

Alix Wood

PowerKiDS
press

Published in 2016 by **Rosen Publishing**
29 East 21st Street, New York, NY 10010

Editor: Eloise Macgregor
Designer: Alix Wood
Consultant: Kevin E. Yates, Fellow of the Royal Astronomical Society

Photo Credits: Cover, 1, 21, 24-25 © Shutterstock; 4 top, 8, © public domain; 4 bottom © Alix Wood/Gregory H. Revera; 5, 18, 20 main image, 25 top , 26-27 © Dollar Photo Club; 6 © Eduemoni; 7 © Alix Wood; 9, 10, 11, 13, 14 top, 15, 16, 20 insets, 22, 23, 25 inset, 27 top inset © NASA; 12 © Gregory H. Revera; 14 bottom © Claudio Santana; 17 top © Steven Hobbs/NASA; 17 bottom © Andrey Pivovarov; 19 © Alix Wood; 27 bottom inset © Photography-Match

Cataloging-in-Publication Data

Wood, Alix.
Why is the moon not a planet? / by Alix Wood.
p. cm. — (The galaxy guides)
Includes index.
ISBN 978-1-4994-0846-1 (pbk.)
ISBN 978-1-4994-0845-4 (6 pack)
ISBN 978-1-4994-0844-7 (library binding)
1. Moon — Juvenile literature. I. Wood, Alix. II. Title.
QB582.W66 2016
523.3—d23

Manufactured in the United States of America

CPSIA Compliance Information: Batch #: WS15PK
For Further Information contact Rosen Publishing, New York, New York at 1-800-237-9932

Contents

What Is the Moon?

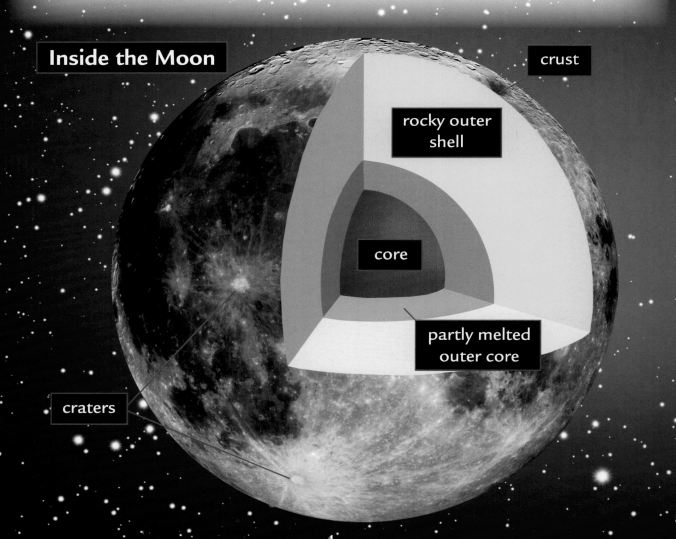

Our Moon was created around 4.5 billion years ago. It is believed that a large object floating in space hit Earth, and chunks of Earth flew off. The pieces then melted together to become the Moon. People think this because the rock on the Moon and on Earth is made of similar material.

moon rock

Inside the Moon

crust

rocky outer shell

core

partly melted outer core

craters

The Moon **orbits** our planet. A journey around an object in space is called an orbit. Orbits happen because objects with a large **mass** in space attract other objects to them. This attraction is called **gravity**.

Moon

Earth

The Moon is a long way from Earth. It is 238,857 miles (384,403 km) away. If you drove from the Moon to Earth at 65 mph (around 100 kph) it would take you 153 days of nonstop driving 24 hours a day!

FACT FILE

What Is the Solar System?

Our solar system has the Sun at its center. Planets, moons, comets, and asteroids all move around the Sun. Objects in space attract other objects to them. This attraction is called gravity. Objects with the most mass have the strongest pull. Objects such as Earth are pulled toward the Sun. Meanwhile, other forces try to pull objects away from the Sun. The forces balance each other out, so Earth circles the Sun. Our Moon orbits Earth, and Earth takes the Moon with it as it orbits the Sun.

the Sun

Earth

the Moon

What Is a Planet?

Aplanet is a body that orbits a star. Scientists only decided on a proper definition for a planet in 2006. It must be large and mostly round. It also must have gathered up most of the other material floating around its own orbit.

Greek stargazers came up with the word "planets" thousands of years ago. They noticed objects that didn't follow a simple path across the sky like stars, and seemed to wander around the sky. The word "planetes" means "wanderer" in Greek.

FACT FILE

The Pluto Problem

Pluto was discovered in 1930 and became the ninth planet in our solar system. In 1991, new, more powerful **telescopes** allowed scientists to discover more objects in space just beyond Pluto. A larger object, Eris, was discovered. There are more objects in the same area that could be larger than Pluto. Are they all planets?

Scientists decided not to have too many planets. In 2006, a group of scientists came up with a definition of what a planet actually was. A part of the definition said a planet must be able to clear the area in its own orbit. Too many other objects float in Pluto's orbit, so it is not a planet anymore, it is a dwarf planet!

Pluto

HANDS-ON SCIENCE

Make a Model of the Sun, Earth, and Moon

You will need: a paper plate, three brass fasteners, some cardboard, crayons or colored pencils

Cut two strips of cardboard, one slightly longer than the paper plate's width, and one around a third as long as the first strip. Cut two cardboard circles; make Earth much smaller than the paper plate Sun. Make the Moon about a quarter the size of Earth. Color them in. Ask an adult to help you push a brass fastener through Earth's center and one end of both strips of cardboard. Attach the Sun to the other end of the long strip, and the Moon to the other end of the smaller strip of cardboard using the fasteners.

the Moon

Earth

the Sun

Look at your model of the Sun, Earth, and Moon. Then look at the definition of a planet on the notepad on the right. Can the Moon be a planet?

A planet must...
1) orbit the Sun (or a star)
2) have enough gravity to turn itself almost **sphere**-shaped like a soccer ball
3) have enough gravity to "clear the neighborhood" around its orbit

How Does the Moon Affect Earth?

The Moon's gravity pulls at Earth. This pull causes a rise and fall in the oceans, known as the **tides**. Earth would be a less stable place to live, too, without the Moon. The Moon's gravity helps slow down Earth's wobble as it orbits the Sun.

Have you ever been to the ocean and wondered why the tide goes in and out? As Earth turns, the Moon pulls at the ocean water directly beneath it, causing the water to rise. A similar rise in sea level occurs on the opposite side of the Earth, where the water bulges out as a result of Earth spinning. At those points on Earth there is a high tide. Six hours later, when Earth has turned 90 degrees, there is a low tide at those points.

a lighthouse at low tide

the same lighthouse at high tide

Ocean Tides

low tide

the Sun

Moon's gravitatonal pull

high tide

Earth

high tide

e Moon

low tide

What Would Happen If We Had No Moon?

If we had no moon the seas would be much calmer. The bulge of water would follow the Sun instead. The Sun is around 400 times further from us than the Moon though, so its pull would be much fainter, and high tide would be around noon every day. The tides help to move **nutrients** around our oceans and lakes. Without strong tides many species that live in water may not survive.

Earth is quite a stable planet, so the weather isn't too extreme. Because of this, life on Earth has been able to flourish. The Moon acts as a stabilizer. At present Earth is tilted at 23.4 degrees as it orbits the Sun. It follows a slightly **elliptical** orbit, a little like the shape of an egg. With no Moon, the angle of our tilt would become unstable. This would affect our seasons and give us more extreme weather as we orbited the Sun.

Why Does the Moon Change Shape?

The Moon is always really a sphere. It can seem to be a different shape, or sometimes disappear altogether, because we see its lit half from different angles as the Moon orbits us.

The inner circle shows how the Sun lights the Moon during its orbit. The outer circle shows what the Moon looks like to us on Earth at that position.

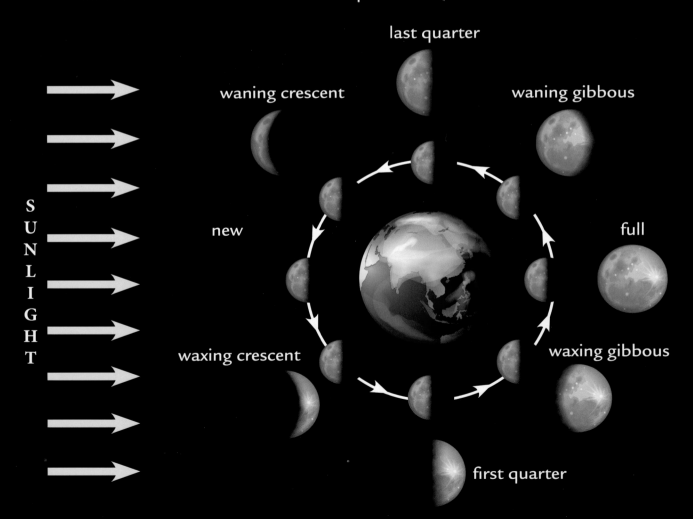

SUNLIGHT

last quarter

waning crescent

waning gibbous

new

full

waxing crescent

waxing gibbous

first quarter

How Does the Moon Shine?

We only see the Moon in the night sky because it is lit up by the Sun. It has no light inside itself, since it is made of rock. As the Moon moves around the Earth, we see its lit half from different angles. This is what produces the changing shapes, known as the **lunar phases.** The Moon takes one month to travel all the way around Earth. In that time, what we see changes from a thin crescent to a full moon and back again to a crescent.

HANDS-ON SCIENCE

Create Your Own Lunar Phase Experiment

You will need: two people, a desk lamp, a swivel chair, a Ping-Pong ball, and a skewer

Ask an adult to stick the skewer through the Ping-Pong ball. It may help if they heat the skewer. Secure the ball in place. The ball is the Moon. Get one person to sit on the swivel chair. They are Earth. Place the desk lamp on a table, shining toward the chair. This is the Sun. The other person holds the "Moon" by its skewer and walks around the chair, as though they are orbiting Earth. The person in the chair swivels around to follow them as they orbit. Have a practice with the lights on to check there is nothing you can trip over. Then turn off the lights. Take turns being "Earth" and see the different phases of the Moon come alive on the Ping-Pong ball!

Why Do We Only See One Side of the Moon?

Have you ever noticed that you only ever see one side of the Moon? You might think it is because the Moon doesn't **rotate**, but it does. The Moon takes the same time to spin once on its axis as it does to orbit the Earth, meaning that its far side is forever turned away from us. Our familiar view of the Moon is pictured right.

near side

The dark patches on the near side of the Moon are called **"maria,"** which is Latin for "seas." Early astronomers mistook them for actual seas. They are really volcanic plains made up of a rock known as basalt.

far side

South Pole-Aitken basin

In 1959, the Soviet Union probe Luna 3 took the first images of the far side of the Moon. It looks very different from the near side. Only one percent of its surface is maria, the rest is covered in **craters**. It also has one of the largest, oldest marks from **impact** in the solar system, the South Pole-Aitken basin. Roughly 1,500 miles (2,414 km) in diameter and 8 miles (13 km) deep, it looks like a slightly darker bruise covering the bottom third of the Moon.

FACT FILE

How Does the Moon Only Show One Side?

The time it takes the Moon to revolve is the same amount of time it takes the Moon to orbit Earth, which means we always see the same side. If you were on the Moon, you would always see Earth in roughly the same place in the sky, too!

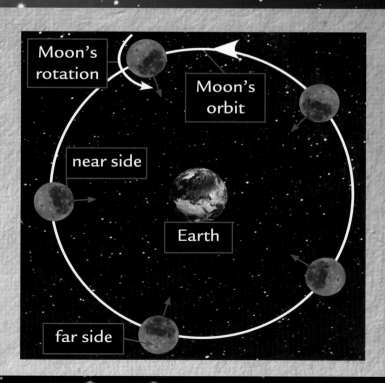

Moon's rotation

Moon's orbit

near side

Earth

far side

Why Does the Moon Sometimes Turn Orange?

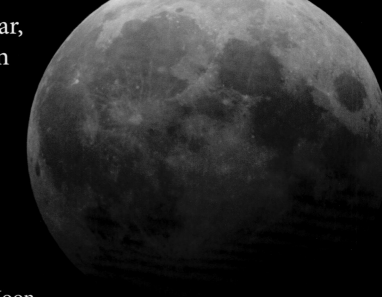

Up to three times a year, when the Moon is on exactly the opposite side of Earth to the Sun, we experience a **lunar eclipse**. The Moon slowly changes to a dark orange color. How does this happen?

During a total lunar eclipse the Moon passes through the Earth's shadow. At the start of the eclipse the Moon gradually gets darker. All of a sudden it changes color, usually to a dark purple or orange color. After a few minutes the process reverses and the Moon gets lighter again until it is back to normal.

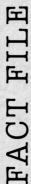

FACT FILE

Where Does the Orange Glow Come From?

During a lunar eclipse some sunlight is able to pass through the Earth's **atmosphere** and gives the Moon an orange glow. Dust in Earth's atmosphere acts like a filter, only letting red and orange light through to the Moon. The same thing happens on Earth after a major **volcanic eruption**. Dust in the atmosphere affects the colors we see in the sky during sunset (right). We can have really beautiful sunsets for months afterwards.

HANDS-ON SCIENCE

Make a Lunar Eclipse!

You will need: a flashlight, an orange, a piece of cardboard, a stick, a piece of clay or Plasticine, some tape

Place the flashlight on a table. This is your Sun. Place the orange around a foot (30 cm) in front. The orange represents Earth. Line up the flashlight's beam so it hits the orange. You may need to raise the orange to achieve this using some clay. Cut out a circle of cardboard that is slightly smaller than the orange, and tape it to the stick. This circle is your Moon. Move the circle using the stick through the shadow created by the orange. You will see your Moon go dark in the shadow. See if you can create a total eclipse.

Sun   Earth   Moon

The Moon doesn't disappear all of a sudden during a total lunar eclipse because Earth's shadow, like all shadows, isn't all completely dark. The lighter part of Earth's shadow is called the "penumbra," and the dark part is called the "umbra." A penumbral lunar eclipse is when the Moon only passes through the lighter part of Earth's shadow. A partial lunar eclipse is when only part of the Moon passes through the darkest part of Earth's shadow. A total lunar eclipse occurs when the entire Moon passes through the darkest part of Earth's shadow. In the diagram above you can see the darker umbra in the center of the shadow.

Do Other Planets Have Moons?

M any other planets have their own moons. There are 146 known moons in our solar system. Moons come in all shapes and sizes. Most are round like ours, but the two moons that orbit Mars look more like small, irregular-shaped **asteroids**.

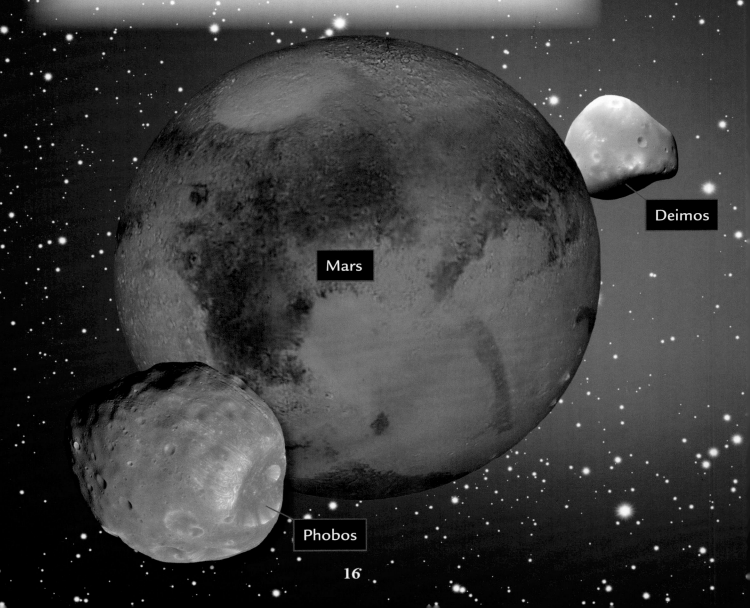

Deimos

Mars

Phobos

Could We Live On a Moon?

FACT FILE

Titan is Saturn's largest moon and the second largest moon in our solar system. Titan has a planet-like dense atmosphere, thought to be much like Earth's atmosphere was a long time ago. Titan has lakes and seas made from liquid gas. It is the only other world in the solar system that has stable liquids on its surface. Titan also has liquid gas rivers and even rain! Sunlight is quite dim on Titan though, so it is very cold. Some scientists believe that in the distant future people could live on Titan. When the Sun increases in temperature near the end of its life, Titan's temperature could be warm enough for stable oceans to exist on the surface. Then conditions on Titan could be similar to Earth's.

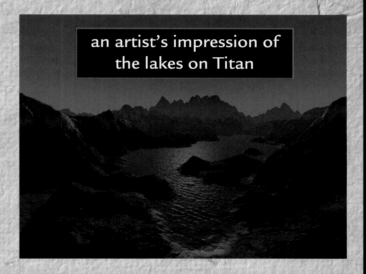

an artist's impression of the lakes on Titan

Titan is surrounded by an orange haze that kept its surface a mystery for Earth's scientists. In 2005, the European Space Agency's *Huygens* lander probe reached Titan on board NASA's *Cassini* orbiter and landed on its surface. It sent back some amazing images.

Titan's orange haze

Could Earth Have More Than One Moon?

Space scientists believe Earth already has other objects that orbit it like a moon does. In 2006, scientists studying the skies in Arizona noticed a mysterious body orbiting the Earth. The object turned out to be a tiny asteroid. It was captured by Earth's gravity in September 2006 and orbited us until June 2007.

Scientists now believe that there is at least one other natural **satellite** orbiting Earth at any one time. The objects usually stay in orbit for around 10 months, and generally complete three orbits around the planet before breaking free.

asteroid

Earth

These temporary satellites may not be moons, but they are very interesting for space scientists. It would be exciting if humans could visit an asteroid. It would be very challenging to reach most asteroids, but if an asteroid was in temporary orbit around the Earth it would be a much easier target. Because most asteroids have never melted like the planets, the material they contain has remained almost unaltered since the formation of the solar system! They are like time capsules holding the chemistry of the early solar system. Scientists would love to examine an asteroid.

HANDS-ON SCIENCE

Make Your Own Edible Asteroids!

You will need: an adult to help you, two medium potatoes, 2 pieces of butter or margarine, pinch of salt and pepper, saucepan, potato masher, mixing bowl, cookie sheet, oven

Asteroids aren't really edible, but these are fun to make! Turn on your oven to 375° Fahrenheit (190° Celsius). Ask an adult to help you cook two potatoes and mash them. Allow to cool. Rub some of the butter on the cookie sheet. Add the rest of the butter, salt, and pepper to the mashed potatoes and mix well. Add some milk if it is too dry, or a little flour if too wet. Shape a handful of mashed potatoes into an asteroid shape. Poke dents in it to create craters. Put your asteroids on the cookie sheet. Place in the hot oven for 20 to 25 minutes, until brown. Remove the tray using oven mitts, allow to cool a little, and eat!

The Sun rises in the morning and sets in the evening. The Moon rises and sets at a different time every day. The new moon starts off in line with the Sun. It rises with the Sun, follows it across the sky, and sets with the Sun. We can't see the new moon as it is too close to the Sun's glare and its lit side faces away from us.

Over the month the Moon starts to lag more and more behind the Sun, by around 50 minutes a day. By first quarter, the Moon is six hours behind the Sun. It rises in the middle of the day and sets in the middle of the night. At full moon, the Moon is opposite the Sun and 12 hours behind it, so it rises as the Sun is setting and sets at sunrise. Look at the times the Moon rises and sets below. Can you guess around what time of day this photo must have been taken?

Rises: 6 a.m.
Sets: 6 p.m.

Rises: 3 a.m.
Sets: 3 p.m.

Rises: midnight
Sets: noon

Rises: 9 p.m.
Sets: 9 a.m.

Rises: 6 p.m.
Sets: 6 a.m.

Rises: 3 p.m.
Sets: 3 a.m.

Rises: noon
Sets: midnight

Rises: 9 a.m.
Sets: 9 p.m.

The Moon's brightness changes during its orbit. A full moon is brightest. Before and after a new moon we only see a sliver of light. We can sometimes see the rest of the Moon faintly, too. This is caused by **earthshine**. The Moon's dark area is lit by light reflecting off Earth.

On the Moon, where there is no atmosphere, you are able to see the stars in the daytime as well as at night.

HANDS-ON SCIENCE

Why Is It Easier for Our Eyes to See Stars at Night?

You will need: cardboard box, skewer, flashlight, sheet of white paper, tape

Punch some holes using the skewer into one side of a cardboard box. You may want to ask an adult to help. Glue a sheet of white paper on the outside. Place the lit flashlight inside the box and switch off the room's lights. Lit from the inside the holes are like stars in the night sky, and can be seen clearly. Now switch on a light in the room. Can you still see the stars?

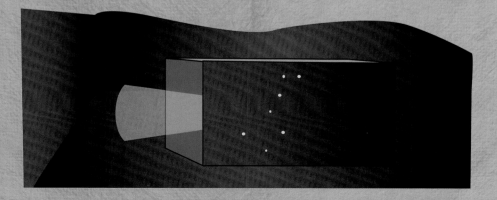

The Moon is the only place besides Earth that people have walked on. In 1969, Apollo 11 landed on the Moon. Commander Neil Armstrong became the first man to walk on the surface of the Moon.

Eugene Cernan walking on the Moon in 1972. He was the last man to walk on the Moon. He and Harrison Schmitt drove on the Moon, too, in a lunar rover buggy.

A Footprint on the Moon

The Moon has no atmosphere, so the Moon doesn't experience weather like we have on Earth. There is no wind or rain that might wear away the dusty surface. This means that footprints left on the Moon by Apollo astronauts will remain visible for millions of years! In 2011, NASA's Lunar Reconnaisance Orbiter took photographs of the disturbed dust where the astronauts had walked and tire tracks left by missions back in the 1960s and 1970s!

Buzz Aldrin's footprint on the Moon

The Saturn V rocket carrying the Apollo 11 spacecraft lifts off from Kennedy Space Center, Florida.

There were space missions before Apollo 11, but this was the first mission to actually land people on the Moon. The crew took a while to find a suitable landing site. When the lander finally touched down, they only had about 20 seconds worth of fuel left! They carried cameras, and broadcast TV pictures of themselves stepping onto the surface of the Moon. Around 600 million people around the world tuned in to watch this historic moment!

The Moon is not a friendly environment for people. There is no **oxygen** to breathe, no food, and no water. It is too hot in the day and too cold at night. Small rocks called micrometeoroids fly around at high speed. Our bodies would find it hard to cope with the different gravity and lack of air pressure on the Moon, too.

FACT FILE

What Our Body Needs

Our bodies are used to Earth's gravity. If gravity is too strong we can't move. If gravity is too weak our muscles waste away.

If we live somewhere with less pressure our bodies puff up. If we have too much pressure our bodies collapse.

Human beings need a body temperature of around 98.6° Fahrenheit (37° Celsius). At just a few degrees higher or lower, we can die from the cold or die from being too hot.

We need to breathe oxygen. If the air contains too little, we'll die.

On the Moon

The Moon has six times less gravity than Earth. Our muscles and bones would weaken.

On the Moon, we would need pressurized space suits or buildings to survive.

Moon temperatures reach 266° Fahrenheit (130° Celsius) and fall to -274° Fahrenheit (–170° Celsius).

There is no oxygen on the Moon.

No one who has been to the Moon could have survived without a space suit. Space suits protect astronauts from extreme temperatures. Their backpacks supply astronauts with oxygen to breathe. They hold water to drink during spacewalks, too. The suit keeps astronauts from being injured by flying rocks. Space suits help protect astronauts from some low energy radiation. A gold-tinted visor filters the bright sunlight, too.

Scientists are always looking at ways that we could one day live on the Moon, however. There is oxygen in Moon rock that we could use to create oxygen to breathe. There are also large, deep pits on the Moon. Living in these could protect us from micrometeroids and radiation. We could use the Sun to create energy. Then we could use that energy to break down water ice that exists deep in the Moon's craters. With water we could then grow our own food.

large pit on the Moon

Can We Learn About Earth from the Moon?

The Moon may not be a planet but we can still learn a lot about Earth by studying the Moon. Earth and the Moon are close neighbors, so whatever happened to the Moon throughout its history also happened to our planet.

Around four billion years ago a large number of asteroids hit the Moon, Earth, and other planets. Many craters on the Moon date from this time. Unlike craters on Earth, they have not been worn away by weather and events like volcanic eruptions. There are 1,700 craters on the Moon. When the Moon was suffering these impacts, so was Earth. Since Earth is four times as big as the Moon, it may have had even more impacts. It is a larger target and has stronger gravity. Earth's atmosphere would have helped protect it from smaller objects' hits, however.

By studying the Moon's craters, scientists can figure out what happens when objects strike the surface of a planet or moon. Meteor Crater in Arizona is one of Earth's best preserved craters. Even so, it has been partly filled with debris and the earth thrown out of the crater on impact, known as **ejecta**, has mostly worn away.

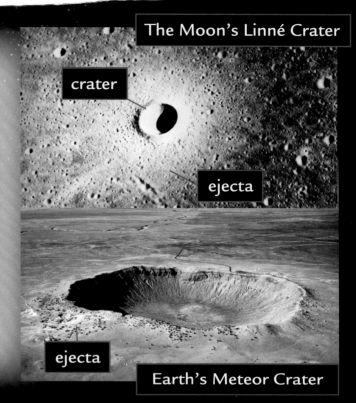

The Moon's Linné Crater

crater

ejecta

ejecta

Earth's Meteor Crater

HANDS-ON SCIENCE

Study Your Own Moon Crater

Meteor Crater is about 4,000 feet (1,219 m) across and 570 feet (174 m) deep. Do you think that was the size of the meteor that crashed there?

You will need: deep tray, flour, cocoa powder, small stone, sieve

Fill the pan halfway up with the flour. Sieve a thin layer of cocoa powder on top. Drop the stone into the flour tray. Is the crater it made the same size as the stone or bigger? Did you get any ejecta around the crater?

Galaxy Quiz

Are you a galaxy genius? Test your skills with this quiz and see if you know your eclipses from your full moons!

1. Which of these statements is correct?
   a) Objects with a large mass attract other objects to them
   b) Objects with a large mass don't attract other objects to them

2. Pluto is a planet.
   a) True
   b) False

3. How does the Moon cause the tides?
   a) The light from the Moon moves the water
   b) The Moon's gravity pulls the ocean water as it passes over it
   c) The Moon warms the seas

4. What shape is the Moon?
   a) Crescent shaped
   b) A semicircle
   c) A sphere

5. What are "maria"
   a) Volcanic areas on the Moon that look like seas
   b) Large craters
   c) Moon buggies

6. We only ever see one side of the Moon from Earth.
   a) True
   b) False

7. When the Moon passes through Earth's shadow, it
   is called
   a) An ejecta
   b) An eclipse
   c) A full moon

8. What is Titan?
   a) A spaceship
   b) A planet
   c) One of Saturn's moons

9. Is the Moon only in our sky at nighttime?

10. Who was the first man to walk on the Moon?
   a) Neil Armstrong
   b) Eugene Cernan
   c) Harrison Schmitt

Glossary

asteroids
(AS-teh-roydz)
Small bodies made of rock and iron that travel around the Sun.

atmosphere (AT-muh-sfeer)
The gases around an object in space. On Earth this is air.

craters (KRAY-turz)
Large holes on a moon or planet.

earthshine (URTH-shyn)
Where the Moon's dark area is slightly lit by sunlight reflecting from Earth's surface.

ejecta (E-ject-tuh)
Matter that has been thrown out as a result of an impact.

elliptical (ih-LIP-tih-kul)
Shaped like an oval.

gravity (GRA-vih-tee)
The force that attracts objects to move toward each other. The bigger an object is, the more gravity it has.

impact (IM-pakt)
The action of one object coming forcibly into contact with another.

lunar eclipse
(LOO-ner ih-KLIPS)
When the Moon appears darkened as it passes into the Earth's shadow.

lunar phases (LOO-ner FAYZ-ez)
The different shapes of the Moon as seen from Earth.

maria (MAH-ree-uh)
Dark regions on the surface of the Moon.

mass (MAS)
The amount of matter in something.

nutrients (NOO-tree-ents)
Food that a living thing needs to live and grow.

orbits (OR-bitz) Moves in a circular path.

oxygen (OK-sih-jen)
A gas that has no color or taste and is necessary for people and animals to breathe.

rotate (ROH-tayt) To move in a spinning motion.

satellite (SA-tih-lyt) An object that circles a planet in space.

sphere (SFEER)
An object that is shaped like a ball.

telescopes (TEH-leh-skohpz)
Tools used to collect light from distant objects so they can be seen in greater detail.

tides (TYDZ) The daily rise and fall of the ocean.

volcanic eruption
(vol-KA-nik ih-RUP-shun)
When magma comes through a crack in Earth's crust.

Further Information

Books

Landau, Elaine. *The Moon* (True Books: Space). New York, NY: Children's Press, 2008.

Lawrence, Ellen. *The Moon* (Zoom into Space). New York, NY: Bearport, 2014.

Due to the changing nature of Internet links, PowerKids Press has developed an online list of websites related to the subject of this book. This site is updated regularly. Please use this link to access the list:
www.powerkidslinks.com/tgg/moon

Index

Answers
1. a)
2. b)
3. b)
4. c)
5. a)
6. a)
7. b)
8. c)
9. No, it is there in the daytime too
10. a)